C000136192

AND SO SHE CHOSE

AND SO SHE CHOSE

JADINE LYDIA

And So She Chose copyright © 2021 by Jadine Lydia.
All rights reserved.
No part of this book may be reproduced in any manner
whatsoever without written permission.

Cover Design: Illuminate Design
Editor: Heather Grace Stewart

ISBN: 978-1-9196223-0-9 paperback
ISBN: 978-1-9196223-1-6 hardcover
ISBN: 978-1-9196223-2-3 eBook

www.jadinelydia.com

To all the women who have ever
doubted themselves,

———————————————

and to those willing to rise in love.

———————————

HER CONTENTS

infinite

'**And so she chose.** To be happy, to be healthy, to be **sexy**, to be **stealthy.**'

JADINE LYDIA

AND SO SHE CHOSE

And so she chose
to be happy, to be healthy,
to be sexy, to be stealthy.
To throw her hands in the air
and dance naked under the stars,
to give love, to spread joy,
to play with Venus and Mars.
To trust the divine
has a much bigger plan,
and when the time is right,
he will fall right into her hands.
And until that time she continues to pour
pure love and devotion into every pore.
Until she drips in joy and bathes in play,
and devours every moment,
until her last dying day.

pure love

SHE CALLS

And so, she wailed.
The soft sound of a siren
calling her home.
She cried,
long tears of a stormy sea,
her hazy gaze, leading her astray,
a myriad of turquoise
laced with soft palettes of grey.
Lovingly, longingly,
she swept her soul,
through channels, through tides,
through ebbs and flow.
Raging waters,
and rugged rocks,
her fears and worries
tumbled and rocked.
And suddenly,
as if by magic,
the sea sat still.
Her palette cleared,
she lifted her gaze
to see her light being
stand tall in the waves.
Beckoning her to come home.

light being

AFTERGLOW

She dusted grey chalk from her skin
and black dust from her heart.
Cobwebs flew skyward,
and feathers flew north.
Up and up and up,
she floated.
A lightness, a brightness,
a newfound love.
For all that she had
and all that she was.
The sky, the sun,
the moon, her love.
Her touch, her taste,
the sky above.
The path was clear,
and so, she chose.
To begin,
again.

feathers

WILD COFFEE

She percolated her thoughts,
slow and steady.
Drip by drip by drip.
Squeezing every ounce of her indispensable
imagination,
into her pot of life.
Tea leaves scattered wildly,
conjuring up the most unthinkable things.
Dregs of coffee swept through her soul,
dark, hazy and high.
She took one last delicious sip,
and let wisdom and wonder
sink into her cup half empty.
Or was it half full?
And then, she realised.
Every thought had meaning,
and every word spoke mattered.
And so she chose
to percolate her thoughts.
Drip by drip by drip.
Refining her texture
into a well-ground life,
in which she created every bitter moment
and each exquisite taste.
Her life, her way.
Her day.

percolate

INCANDESCENT LOVE

———————————

She wrote something about nothing
as her feet squelched incandescently
into the mulch below.
Silently crippled by her infinite eternity,
she felt soft, silver petals fall upon her skin.
A pink glow, guiding her to her next
discovery,
the truth behind all matter.
Moss delicately and decadently ate away
at her outer skin,
feeding upon all that she had shed.
And down to her bare bones and bark,
she knew.
The death of her would be her making.
And so she mulched on,
into the woods of eternity,
and danced beneath the leaves of love.

eternity

> HER LOVE

'**Her heart wrung.**
A flood of black matter.
Ring after ring after ring.
As her tears fell softly,
onto **frayed heartstrings.**'

JADINE LYDIA

HONEYCOMB LOVE

She was yellow.
Yellow like honey.
Oh honey goodness,
plastered on the walls.
Warm, thick, mellow,
she melted in her madness.
Sweet with delight.
Oh sweet madness,
you are my honey.
My sweet, sweet honey.
Your golden nectar holds,
a dear space in my heart.
Honeycomb hexagons
and sweet pollen love.
You are enough,
she whispered.
You are enough.
My honeycomb love.

honey

THE PINK HEART

Her heart ached.
A slow pulse of an infinite purge.
Heaving, hollowing, holding.
All that she had lost,
in his wake.

Her heart purged.
A tumultuous amount of tar.
Swirling, whirling, stirring.
Seaweed from the depths of her darkest matter,
tainting the glow of her green goddess blood.

Her heart stung.
A throbbing, lashing line.
As the explicit and undeniable truth rose
to the surface of a sunken sea.
A web of lies and deceit.

Her heart wrung.
A flood of black matter.
Ring after ring after ring.
As her tears fell softly,
onto frayed heartstrings.

purge

HER LOVE

Her heart went numb.
A vital organ frozen in red,
flatlining as ferocious fear
ran through her veins,
seeping through her system.

Finally, her heart sang.
As pale, pink quartz,
cleansed, cleared and caressed,
the channel of love,
as her love walked away.

numb

POLAR ATTRACTION

———————————————

She surrendered,
gently, quietly, receptively,
in the feminine way.

She played,
curiously, compulsively, seductively,
in her feminine play.

She called,
lightly, softly, wildly,
in her womanly way.

She danced,
fiercely, freely and fearlessly,
in her divine play.

She loved every risky polarity,
of each and every day.

BODY OF LOVE

She awoke
to the reality that this day
was like no other.
Something had shifted.
She had risen
above and beyond
all expectations.
Above this minuscule existence
into something quite profound.
Expansive, elevated,
in her evolution;
rising high,
and sinking low.
A body of pain,
a shimmering glow.
She shifted
her madness
into melodies,
her sadness
into symphonies.
No ends
into pathways,
all the way home;
into her body of love.

evolution

EMBODIED LOVE

She radiated love.
Love like no other love
she had ever felt before.
It was a vibration
pounding in her heart,
exploding through her veins.
Pulsating waves of inspiration;
infusing every little cell
in her ever-expanding body,
with full-blown bliss.
This love was her love.
The one she had chosen,
from the depths of her soul
and the fire in her heart.
This love had been waiting
on the back burner
for a long, long time.
And finally,
she had aligned.
This was her love.

veins

> HER LIGHT

'She let herself **crumble** into
the **ashes** of night,
then she rose as a **phoenix**,
radiating her **pure white** light.'

JADINE LYDIA

phoenix

AGE OF AQUARIUS

In the age of Aquarius,
she was brought back to life.
With white pearls around her neck,
and a trident of turquoise love.
She swam in the oceans,
and bathed in ancient ruins,
she held a locket to her heart,
golden with pure wisdom.
She let her lungs fill,
with water and white light,
and sprayed fountains of beauty
against pale pink, cloud-washed skies.
She called in the light,
her matrix shifting times,
a Piscean priestess,
a warrior of the light.
This was her time;
in the ocean of life.
This was her time,
in the life of paradise.

pearls

THE WHITE ROSE

The white rose
stood tall with poise and grace.
Her skin glows
cotton and milky silk interlaced.
Perfect, pretty, poignant,
worth a stop and stare.
Dusty rose cheekbones,
painted with delightful care.
Delicate and dainty,
she sips her sweet green tea,
a bitter pout, a pursed-lip vow,
her little finger held in glee.
For this white rose knows
one simple way to be.
Pretty, perfect, poignant;
so elegant is she.

grace

DAISY LIGHT

———————————

She danced delicately,
as soft as a daisy.
Pretty, perfect petals,
falling to the ground.
Crisp, white in colour,
she called in her pure clarity.
A warm yellow centre,
golden nectar to her honey.
Green, green grass,
holding her insanity.
She drank her juicy droplets,
one by one by one,
sipping from the heavens,
she filled her heart and lungs.
She blossomed, she bloomed,
and faced the rising sun,
in her pure white composure,
she bathed in eternal light.

petals

PLASTIC MACKINTOSH

The yellow coat, she wore.
A plastic mackintosh,
varnished with the smell of spring,
a daffodil in disguise.
She dipped in and out of the crowds,
spreading her happy go lucky light,
in the free-spirited way
in which one gives,
one loves,
and one simply does.
Because it's the only way.
She flitted in and out,
like a bumblebee,
harvesting her sweet nectar.
She picked up, dropped off
and revelled in the madness
of an ever-changing world.
A world in which we bounce,
reflect and retract
in a flurry of potent pollen,
convulsions of effervescent energy.
A world where we can choose,
to reflect, retract or restore,
the sun rays beneath the surface,
of every inquisitive interaction.
The yellow within us all.

pollen

VIOLET FLAME

The flame within her burned so bright.
She tore down stars,
and brought galaxies to light.
She coursed cosmos and ether
from her violet heart stream,
her aura alight,
with sun and moonbeams.
She scattered the sky,
with green moldavite,
dazzling white showers
and vast rays of light.
And in this explosion,
she could not be tamed,
for it was her supernova,
it was her violet flame.

supernova

> HER BEING

'When
darkness clouded her
infinite **being,**
she **gazed** into the night.
For that **tiny speck** of
golden nectar, that
would be her **guiding
light.**'

JADINE LYDIA

nectar

PEARLY WISDOM

She sat still.
Balancing in a particular manner,
on the very edge of existence.
Questioning the very point,
of this peculiar reality.
In which she knew nothing,
she had decided,
about anything.
Except, what she had been told.
And with this spark of pearly wisdom,
she emptied her mind,
carelessly and
curiously,
of all that she knew.
And chuckled,
as she was lost for words,
for she could now not find the language,
nor comprehension
to contemplate such things.

Only a vast emptiness,
filled with nothingness.
No words, no preconceptions,
no deviations.
Only, a blank space.
Or was it white?
She sat, in her peculiar manner,
for a matter of moments
enjoying a dumbfounded escape,
into an otherwise,
unknown reality.
In which, quite frankly,
nothing really mattered at all.

blank

TWISTED PURPLE

She sang her blues.
A medley of twisted purple,
stirred lightly with a wooden fork.
Juicy, ripe and ready to harvest;
her sorrows, her blessings,
her countless beginnings.
Her heart broken yet bursting,
with endless endings.
And her wheel of life,
turned again.
She relished the ripeness,
despite the slight twang.
And she knew.
Her purple tarnished fingers
would reap what they had sown.
For it could only be so.

blues

CHASING CLARITY

She woke up feeling different.
Not good, not bad, not ugly.
But not quite the same.
She couldn't quite put her finger
on what was exactly different;
it was as if a shift in perspective,
had happened so suddenly,
she was now unsure
of her very own eyes.
Was she seeing clearly?
Or was she chasing clarity?
She did not know.
It was only different.
The rising feeling
that something should be wrong.
But maybe, finally,
she had got it right.
There was no right or wrong.
Only different.
And so she dared,
to live each moment
just as it was.
Whether it was different
from the last,
or different from the next.
Different she did.

ugly

DIRTY ROOTS

───────────

She was a radical being.
Want not, dread knot.
Barefoot wanderer,
planting her soul,
in a muddy pot of life.
Hands in soil,
roots on earth,
feeding the five thousand
with her simple spread;
chutney and crackers,
olive pips
and plant medicine.
She fed them all.
Watering every last being,
with her earth-born soul.

mud

THE HONEST SELF

She tried to be honest.
At least most of the time,
with others and the world around her.
How she thought, what she felt
and what she did.
And then there was the other.
The part of her that pretended,
that what she really wanted,
didn't matter.
Because this was enough.
Or was it?
She stuffed this feeling down
into her flighty heart,
only for it to rise,
and rise again.
She was an honest person,
she told herself.
To be honest with others,
was an easy pleasure.
But to be honest with herself,
was another matter.
In her truthful dishonesty,
she felt a strange sensation
strangling her stomach.
She churned, uncomfortably.
Was this enough?

down

FOREST GREEN

She lay
with her skin on the earth,
and roots at her feet.
Dirty and delicious,
pure feminine peat.
She wrapped her body
around the base of her trunk;
teardrops falling,
into the soil of love.
Raindrops scattered,
on her fragile white skin,
pink and bruised,
she lay under her leaves.
She whispered quietly,
her envy and ivy
grew twisted and wildly,
untamed by the roots
strangling her quietly.
She grieved.
Heavy and hollow,
burying her sorrows
beneath earth and soil,
her inner turmoil,
decaying,
piece by piece by piece.

soil

She let herself weep.
And then, she breathed.
Fresh sap seeped into her bones;
bringing new life,
new blood and new love,
to what had always been.
Her naked body,
forever green.

green

ENOUGH SAID

―――――――――――

Stay, she said.
As she whispered from her lungs
and longed from her heart.
Inviting the other,
into a space of surrender.
In which she was willing to give over
the chase, to a subtler space.
In which she lay
naked and bare,
with her truths on the table,
and holes in her heart.
Her wild infatuations,
a mere memory of the past.
As she discovered
what it truly meant
to love another.
To be seen.
To be had.
To be held.
In all her glory,
and all her being.
She was enough.

naked

> HER VOYAGE

'She knew, there was
only **one way out.**
Not over, not under,
but through.
And so she took a **deep breath,**
dived right in and emerged
as something new.'

JADINE LYDIA

emerge

A PURE WHITE MOMENT

She sank deep down into the centre
of her barely beating heart.
And asked why this journey
must voyage so deep into the dark.
A pure, pickled tear
ran down her mottled skin.
Her soul asked silently
when her life would begin again.
And whilst huddled in this darkness,
cradled by her heart,
she found a void of vastness,
to illuminate with stars.
And in this pure, white moment,
of existential bliss,
she discovered that all there was,
was all there ever really is.
And so from that day forward
she vowed to embrace it all,
to pickle every teardrop
and save the best for years to come.
For when it was truly time
for her to shine her light,
she would paint every teardrop
as an illuminated sky.

teardrop

THE PURPLE THISTLE FLOWER

—————————

The thorns they prickle,
a needle to her skin.
Persistent in their nature,
they sting again and again.

Her blood thickens,
she feels that there's no hope,
as she settles for another day,
on the same old prickly road.

Until, one day,
she stops to sift and sigh.
And a purple thistle flower
gently catches her eye.

Amongst the petty prickles,
and the pinpoint stings,
she realises that all hardship,
must give birth to beautiful things.

prickle

For this little flower,
has no soil or rain.
Only its tiny self,
in big, old barren terrain.

And yet, it flowers
and emanates a glow,
and in this sigh of a breath,
she knew it to be so.

No matter how many cuts,
bruises or prickly stings,
her light would always shine
above all of these things.

shine

TECHNICOLOUR BLUE

She dipped her toe gently,
into a bucket of icy blue.
Hoping to be baptised,
into something clean, bright and new.
Little did she know,
that this alter did deceive,
for it was laced with deadly poison
that would burn, destroy and seize.
And so she gazed at her toe,
as her skin began to dissolve,
and made a wary choice,
only for the brave and the bold.
She picked up the bucket,
and poured it over her head,
she let her skin dissolve
and delighted at what was left.
A body of technicolour tie-dye;
pink, white and blue,
she revelled in the almighty,
and the truth that she now knew.
For pain was inevitable
and no baptise would wipe her clean.
But if she filled her thoughts with colour,
safe she would always be.

burn

THE LONELY HEART

———————————

Her heart ached.
Heavy from loneliness,
full from fear.
A seam of sadness
stitched, split and spat,
thick black tar
on her pale pink lungs.
Hungry for love,
her stomach rumbled
a thunderous roar;
an empty void.
Lightning hit her central system,
sparks burnt every last synapse
and she screamed.
'Let me be seen!'
The heavens opened,
her word was heard,
and suddenly, she could see.
Beneath her loneliness,
was stitched her fear.
Beneath her fear,
was etched her hunger.
Beneath her hunger,
was sown her soul,
just waiting to be seen.

stitch

RAZOR-SHARP

She lay, shattered
into a thousand, tiny pieces;
sharp edges searing,
her paper-thin skin.
Opaque glass cast with a dirty mist,
her last drop of water delicately placed
on the rim of which her fingertips had rung,
the low chime of a filthy hum.
Around and around and around,
reverberating her pain,
endlessly and relentlessly,
until she dropped.
Yet, in this shattered state,
she vowed to stow her story
and slowly conspired,
to transmute and transpire
her broken glass, into a broken pane.
A stained glass story,
in which her one thousand tiny shatters
became a timeless mosaic,
of perfectly, imperfect pieces;
her razor-sharp light.

glass

> HER KNOWING

'She knew.
Every **little cell** in her body
was on the **right path.**
And so, she let the **elixir of life,**
be her guide.'

JADINE LYDIA

elixir

BONFIRE SKY

She shifted, she sorted, she sighed;
a slight sadness filled her humble heart.
A collection of summer snapshots
to be boxed, stored and kept,
stowed neatly in the attic until the rising of spring.
Autumn drew in and her sentiment took hold;
a warm glow, tainted with the ever-fading sun.
She reminisced;
crispy, baked blackberry pies,
crackling log fires
and cocoa dusted cream.
The winds howled,
the leaves fell,
the earth rumbled.
And in this snapshot
behind a dusty frame,
she waited quietly,
and expectantly,
for the birth of her bonfire sky.

cocoa

WILD WISDOM WONDER

She was a maiden,
in white lamb cotton,
innocence surrounding,
her blue blouse buttons.

Light and breezy,
she danced through daisies,
weaving a crown,
amongst long, golden strands.

Under the sunlight,
she sat in lengthy cotton,
and cried in disdain,
at a red pool of mud.

Oh, what is this?
This pool of agony.
Oh, what is this?
A red pool of love?

She ran home to her mother,
footprints barely touching.
Along dusty, beaten tracks,
eyes frozen like a rabbit.

blouse

HER KNOWING

She threw her white cotton
into the arms of her mother.
And asked how she was living,
because she was surely dying.

Her mother chuckled quietly,
running hot water through her lightly.

You my dear maiden,
are now wild, wisdom wonder.
You my dear maiden,
will one day be a mother.

maiden

THIRSTY WORK

She pressed on;
her foot squeezing every last drop,
of blood-red wine,
from round, juicy bodies.
Sweetness, sweetness,
until suddenly,
it turned.
The bitterness began,
blood-red dripped from her hands.
It was then she knew,
from the skin of her heart
and the flesh of her feet.
There was no going back.
She had reached the final drop,
in her bitter-sweet story.
Another blood poured ending,
turning water into wine,
and wine into water.
She parched.
She drank.
She thirst.

thirst

GOLDEN KINGDOM

She shifted,
left to right, right to left.
Wobbling around her decisions,
her freedom, her intuition,
her kingdom.
In which she knew existed,
but did not yet live in.
Her inner realms
golden with possibility.
Her mind lost,
in absolute uncertainty.
Yet she knew.
She always knew
that she was right,
this was not her life.
It was just another verse
in her freedom song,
in which she had to let go,
and simply move on.
Swiftly.

kingdom

INSATIABLE DESIRE

In an insatiable attempt
to tame her desires,
she prolonged
what she knew,
she would inevitably do,
until a later date.
When the tug at her wires
became so strong
that she could do nothing,
but crumble
into the cave
of self-inflicted pain.
A little fish in the big pond,
of her weary subconscious mind.

tug

> HER POWER

'She stood
frightened, yet
fearless.
Her pupils wide, with
hungry eyes.
And in this contrast,
she knew.
She was at her most
powerful.'

JADINE LYDIA

hungry

SHADOW LOVE

She welcomed her new acquaintance,
the shadow beneath her skin.
Dark ink ran through her veins,
fuelling her deepest, darkest sins.
Her prowling, sensual being,
the animal laced with shame.
Her feisty, assertive priestess,
a goddess with no vain.
Her wrongdoings and guilty pleasures,
all things laced in black.
She held them in her heart
and stirred a love from lack.
For she was whole in her being,
even in the deadliest of sins.
She was whole in her goddess,
in wrongdoings and her wins.
And so she welcomed this acquaintance
and stopped striving for the light.
She truly loved the darkness,
of her unruly shadow side.

THE CHASE

She had been running
for as long as she could remember.
Never settling for too long.

She had been feeling this feeling,
for as long as she could remember.
But she didn't know exactly
where it had come from.

She darted, fiercely in and out
of umpteen circles;
people, places, possibilities.
And then she would stop.

Dead in her tracks,
a deer in the headlights,
frozen in fight or flight.

Only, she would never fight.
Nor, would she flight.
She would just fall.

flight

Back into the chase
from which she was running.
From so-called, nothing.
Or, so she thought.

Until one day, it surfaced.
In all its gnarly glory;
a bear rearing its final frontier.

But she couldn't move,
for it had taken hold.
And now, it was all that she could see,
again and again and again.

So, in one quick breath
she chose to release
this gnarly black truth
from her benevolent being.

And set herself free.

glory

WILD BLAZER

She was a wild one.
Brazen, bold and bloodthirsty.
Craving anything and everything that moved;
a black panther to her prey.
She crept up in locomotion,
stealthy, silky, silent.
Then pounced rapidly
into a black-eyed frenzy,
gorging on their flesh, their blood,
and their bones.
Ripping one limb from the next,
savouring every last morsel
between her blood-red lips.
She feasted, she fed,
and she filled,
her tiny, hungry belly
with meat galore.
Her merciful sins
held no remorse,
for she fed with delight,
to feed her teeny, tiny lives.

stealth

SCATTERED MOMENTS

———————————

Sometimes, she felt scattered.
Like she was in a million places,
with a thousand tiny moments
hashed together,
into a hectic, hazy state.

Sometimes, she felt off-balance.
Like she was being pulled
left, right and centre.

Only she had lost her centre
amongst the chaos and insanity
of a moment less lived;
in sacrifice of a moment yet gained.

She tried so hard
to keep up with the never-ending game.

Always levelling up
to the next expectation,
the next creation,
and the next indentation
in her sparky, yet sunken soul.

chaos

Until finally, one day, she said:
enough is enough!

She burned her bridges
and cut her ties.
She stopped living a life
of bullshit lies.

She scorched fiercely.
She wept wildly.
She rejoiced highly.

And she breathed.

Into the life she had always dreamed.

Simple, light and free.

free

COTTON CANDY

She twisted her little finger
around pastel-coloured curls.
And delighted in her playfulness
as a cotton candy girl.
Sweet in her nature,
with a slight bitter grit,
she held pink clouds on her tongue
and sugar between her lips.
Provocatively pretty,
she giggled with delight,
as the grit beneath her teeth
dissolved into a cotton candy sky.
She batted her long lashes
and gave a little twirl,
as she proclaimed her power proudly
as a sweet, yet sinister girl.
For cotton was her candy,
and candy she did love,
for it gave her the grace of innocence
in her secret, stealthy world.

grit

NUMB FINGERS

She felt numb.
Almost like nothing.
No fear, no pain, no sadness, no heartache.
Just an empty void
of bottomless nothing.
Her fingers bled white
as her heart flat-lined.
One straight bloodline,
beat after beat after beat,
fallen concrete.
She stood in this moment
not grasping reality,
until one sharp pinch
bought her back to life.
Like skin to a knife,
she was alive.
And although she thought
she could not feel everything,
she decided everything was something
and something better than nothing.
The fear, the pain,
the sadness, the heartache,
she welcomed it gladly
and opened the gateway.

pinch

She let it all flood in.
Fiercely, she felt
every last morsel,
until it could no longer bite.
For she was alive.

alive

RED BERRY

She was a red berry kinda girl.
You know the one.
Lips plump, drag in hand.
Curves, contours
and colour pop lipstick,
she smacked, she slapped,
and stole the show.
A vivacious pool
of crushed berry tones.
Nude in complex,
bronzed in character.
Complete and certain,
born to slay.
Sultry and seductive
in her self-assured way.
Lips sealed,
precise in motion
ready to pounce.
Here, now, then.
She owned it all;
her sexy,
her sins.
her sadness.
In her crisp, white suit,
she slayed.

smack

ELECTRIC CLOUD

She was electric.
Impulsive and impatient.
Petrol blue, oil on water.
Silky, smooth and dangerous;
spilt on blood pool eyes.
Live wires ran through her veins
until her cells exploded in one big bang.
Highly charged atoms and electric currents
surged through the sea.
A whirlpool of infinite ecstasy
riding on the very edge
of systematic overwhelm.
Shock waves of light
spread across unlit oceans,
igniting everything in her path.
Her soul burnt into clouds of smoke,
she rose in flames and in fire she choked.
Swirling, swirling, swirling.
To higher and higher heights.
Her oil was her water.
A black pool of life.

oil

HER POWER

RECKLESS WONDER

She glowed.
A shimmer in the night,
roaming free, dark and easy.
Unaware of the shadow
stalking her soul.
She wandered,
aimlessly, fearlessly and recklessly;
like a thief into the night,
stealing gold from their pockets
and silver from their hearts.
She glinted.
The light in her eyes
making them weary, cautious and compulsive;
hungry for more.
And so they followed
in the wake of her shadow.
Only to be devoured
by her devious soul.

gold

> HER BELIEVING

'She swept her **hopes,**
into a **sky full** of dreams.
And let her **faith** deliver,
on a pair of golden
wings.'

JADINE LYDIA

faith

WHITE VALLEY

It was at her disposal.
The almighty force
above, below and within.
Her divine direction,
the precursor,
the lover,
the mother.
Heaven almighty knows
what form she may take.
But she took form,
flooding every river
with her eternal water.
Blessing every mountain,
each valley,
and every forest
with her almighty power.
White and blue,
she swept.

divine

MILKY MEDICINE

A glass of milk
with a few cubes of ice
would make things nice,
she thought.

She loved
her crisp white glass
and the crackle beneath her tongue.
It made her young.

She loved
her faded yellow mug;
a pot of delicious curves.
It made her melt.

She loved
a few pieces of pineapple,
just for the twang.
Yellow ice, how nice,
she thought.

They laughed
at her ridiculous pot of milk.
She cackled back!
My milk is my medicine.
It keeps me strong.

melt

INFINITE WORD

Her eyes told a story
of memories and dreams.
Picture perfect moments,
and those to be seen.
Captured in a blink
and bottled with cloudy love,
envisioned in a breath
and felt with her beating heart.
Her present and unfolding future
undoubtedly are told,
as her past shapes her desires
and new memories evolve.
The creator, the dreamer,
the eternal believer is she,
as she delights in the thoughts
of what she knows could truly be.
For she knew passionately, deeply,
and oh so lovingly so,
that her dreams were white clouds
and her blue sky would surely glow.
For as long as she envisioned
and spoke her holy word,
anything was possible
in her divinely infinite world.

blink

DOVE LIFE

She finally understood.
Everything she had ever wanted
was right at her door.
She clicked, she dropped, she spun.
Her wheel of fortune flew into place
as swiftly as a dove to the sky;
powdering her dreams with notions
that she could really fly.
She kept her wings light
and her feathers soft,
floating her thoughts
into the sky above.
Magic dropped
into her daily living,
her daily doing,
and her daily being.
Until one day,
she stopped
and realised:
she really did
have it all.

dove

SHELLS

Her tiny impulses
said it all
as she rested her eyes
on the rise and the fall.
Creatures of the sand
scuttled beneath her toes,
subtle in movement,
white shells in hand.
Teeny, tiny movements,
shifted in her soul;
guiding her to horizons
yet to unfold.
And so she crept,
like shellfish across the sand.
Listening quietly,
treading lightly,
finding her new home.

subtle

> HER BLISS

'In her world of
paradise,
everything was **bliss.**
Birds sang their
tropical song,
and butterflies kissed
her lips.'

JADINE LYDIA

WHITE DUST

She glittered.
A thousand sparkles
twinkling on a turquoise sea.
She sprinkled
white dust
on tiny pyramids of crystal, clear water,
blessing each wave with eternal bliss.
She floated
light as a feather,
buoyant and bright,
cradled by an ever-moving sea.
She sang;
streaming darkness
from the watery depths,
simply to be free.

dust

DIRTY ORANGE

She sat on her suntrap doorstep,
bare feet, honey glazed, in blue-eyed wonder.
She peeled orange flesh from a juicy body,
tiny, coloured droplets
sticking to her skin.
A bead of sweat trickled
down her wonky spine,
hurdles of bone
in a body of rays.
Sour, a little bit of sweet.
She sucked her segment
and all its juice
into her pink windpipe.
Oh, sweetness.
She tossed her peel
into the overgrown jungle,
returning fruits of the earth
to burnt orange roots.
She spat sour pips
high into the sky,
and watched white seed
bounce on solid concrete,
hungry for auburn growth.
She shuffled and pushed white seed
into the jungle of green,
laughing at the kindness
of her grubby little toe.

jungle

PINK BOTTLED KISSES

On an ink worthy palette
she painted her wildest dreams.
One of hope and love and lust,
and a life by the sea;
of long, rolling waves
shaking her soul,
and stirring her life
into an endless wavy flow.
She dreamt of breath, of life,
of sweet fresh air,
of contrast and longing
and lungs of despair;
of darkness, of clouds,
of pale blue skies,
of pink bottled kisses
and sweet little lies.
Because she could,
she was, and she did.
And so, she lived every second
with her head in her heart,
and her heart in the clouds;
breathing in the life
of her full-blown world.

palette

MOON CHILD

Oh my, oh my,
her mother cried,
as she was born under the moon
of a starlit sky.
Wispy clouds floated
above and beyond;
as the birth of her soul
fell into mother's arms.
And on this dusty moon
the forces that did lay,
brought tenderness and love
in a white cloud of clay.
For her eyes were imprinted
with a soft, silver glow
and each time she looked up,
the angels did know.
That she would follow the waxing,
the waning and the crescent;
and in her gentle midst
be forever present.
For her connection was strong,
and her willpower so pure;
and with her mother's love
she would birth life once more.

starlit

ORANGE SOUL

She burned;
a firecracker in the night.
Her wild ways,
and wistful play
painting stars in the sky.
Music rang,
church bells sang,
and people gathered wide.
To hear her soft white whispers
and orange-tainted life.
She danced above her body,
rhythms in her heart;
she dusted them with colour
and lay her soul amongst the stars.
Guiding, lighting, shining,
she watched over weary souls.
Burning, oh so brightly,
and calling them back home.
Dani lost. Dani love.
Dani life.

wild

ETERNAL GLOW

———————————

In the presense of darkness,
she shone her pure, white light.
A reflection of sunlight
in a vast, open sky.
Held by her heartstrings
and cradled by the stars,
she gazed beyond matter,
to Jupiter and Mars.
She glistened, she twinkled,
and sang to the sea,
turning the changing tides
with effortless flow and ease.
She whispered, she glittered,
and lit dark, heavy skies,
with the eternal glow
of knowing her own light.

moon

Jadine Lydia is an Intuitive Life Coach L.C.H Dip.
Manifestation Maker and Universal Lover & Co-Creator.

She lives on the Cornish Coast in South West England.

Her blog shares her happy-go-lucky, holistic approach to love, laughter and life; inspiring others to deepen their connection to the divine.

She empowers others to take 'intuitive action' towards manifesting their deepest dreams and desires.

Her latest books and self-development courses can be found via her website:

www.jadinelydia.com

 @jadinelydia

Printed in Great Britain
by Amazon

67305405R00047